I0004783

SQL and PL/SQL in Practice Series

Volume 4: The Joy of Applying Subqueries

Djoni Darmawikarta

Copyright © 2016 by Djoni Darmawikarta

Table of Contents

Preface

The Joy of Applying Subqueries, the 4th volume of the *SQL and PL/SQL in Practice* series, is for those who need to learn how to better use subqueries.

A subquery is a **SELECT** statement within another **SQL** statement. Seemingly plain, subquery has variety of options that beginners often overlook their opportunities to solve the requirements for queries and data maintenance.

Assume we have sales and product tables created by the following statements.

```
CREATE TABLE sales (
    product_code    VARCHAR2(10),
    sales_dt        DATE,
    customer_no     VARCHAR2(10),
    quantity        NUMBER,
    sale_price      NUMBER
);

CREATE TABLE product (
    product_code    VARCHAR2(10) PRIMARY KEY,
    product_name    VARCHAR2(15),
    category        VARCHAR2(15),
    price           NUMBER(6,2),
    launch_dt       DATE,
    vendor_no       VARCHAR2(10)
);
```

One of the common uses of a subquery is providing a comparison value in a query's WHERE condition, as shown in the following example SELECT statement. The subquery on line 13 provides the average price as the comparison value in the WHERE condition. A subquery in the WHERE clause is known as nested subquery.

Line 4 -6 is also a subquery. The subquery, which provides the product name from the product table, is a condition of the CASE expression.

```
SELECT
    s.product_code,
        CASE WHEN
            (SELECT product_name
                FROM product
                WHERE product_code = s.product_code
```

```
        ) LIKE 'R%'
    THEN 'Analytics'
    ELSE 'Other'
    END product_class
FROM sales s
WHERE sale_price <= (
    SELECT AVG(price)
    FROM product
);
```

```
 1 ⊟ SELECT
 2       s.product_code,
 3           CASE WHEN
 4               (SELECT product_name
 5                   FROM product
 6                   WHERE product_code = s.product_code)
 7           LIKE 'R%'
 8           THEN 'Analytics'
 9           ELSE 'Other'
10           END product_class
11   FROM sales s
12   WHERE sale_price <=
13           (SELECT AVG(price) FROM product)
14           ;
```

As another example, the following UPDATE statement has two subqueries. The subquery on line 3 - 4 provides the update value, while the other on line 6 – 7 provides the value to be tested for its existence by the EXISTS condition. Notice that while the first subquery has no relationship with the sales table to updated, the second, the customer table is related to sales table on their customer_no columns. The second subquery is called correlated subquery.

```
UPDATE sales s
SET customer_no =
  (SELECT vendor_no FROM product p
  WHERE vendor_NAME = 'Big Store')
WHERE EXISTS
  (SELECT 1 FROM customer c
  WHERE c.customer_no = s.customer_no and c.customer_name = 'Medium
      Store')
;
```

```
1 □ UPDATE sales s
2   SET customer_no =
3     (SELECT vendor_no FROM product p
4     WHERE vendor_NAME = 'Big Store')
5   WHERE EXISTS
6     (SELECT 1 FROM customer c
7     WHERE c.customer_no = s.customer_no and c.customer_name = 'Medium Store')
8   ;
```

A subquery can also be an argument of a function as exemplified in the following query where the subquery on line 5 is an argument of the TO_CHAR function.

```
SELECT * FROM sales
WHERE
    product_code =
    TO_CHAR(
    (SELECT product_code FROM product WHERE product_name = 'Go')
    );
```

```
1 □ SELECT * FROM sales
2   WHERE
3       product_code =
4       TO_CHAR(
5       (SELECT product_code FROM product WHERE product_name = 'Go')
6       );
```

You might already be initiated on the uses of subqueries in the previous three examples, but might not be aware or expect that a subquery can play a role in an analytic windowing clause. (See my other book: Windowing for Analytics)

In the following INSERT statement, for example, the subquery on line 5 – 6 supplies a scalar expression in the starting boundary of the RANGE option. This kind of query, which provides a value for each of its parent query's row is called scalar subquery.

```
INSERT INTO sales_fact
  (SELECT product_code, quantity, sale_price,
      ROUND( AVG (sale_price)
      OVER (ORDER BY quantity RANGE BETWEEN
      (SELECT quantity FROM product
      WHERE product_code = s.product_code)
      PRECEDING AND CURRENT ROW ), 2 )
      win_avg_price
```

```
   FROM sales s
);
```

```
 1 ⊟ INSERT INTO sales_fact
 2      (SELECT product_code, quantity, sale_price,
 3          ROUND( AVG (sale_price)
 4          OVER (ORDER BY quantity RANGE BETWEEN
 5          (SELECT quantity FROM product
 6          WHERE product_code = s.product_code)
 7          PRECEDING AND CURRENT ROW ), 2 )
 8          win_avg_price
 9        FROM sales s
10      );
```

In this book, you will learn subquery from the perspective of the following six roles:

- Participating in conditions
- Generating select list
- Creating virtual table
- Facilitating data maintenance
- Defining view

Knowing where and which way to apply, you will enjoy having subquery in your SQL armory. This book, by way of examples, shows you the variety of ways you can apply subqueries.

To learn the most of this book, you need to have working SQL skill. If you have difficulty following this book, try my other book, the 1st volume of *SQL and PL/SQL in Practice* series: *Learning the Basics in No Time*.

Book Examples

To learn the most out of this book, try the book examples. Set up your own Oracle database and SQL Developer tool to freely and safely try the examples.

You can download free of charge both the database and the tool from the Oracle website. Appendix A is your guide to install the software; Appendix B shows you how to particularly use SQL Developer to try the book examples.

Chapter 1: Participating in Conditions

A subquery can be part of a condition. In this chapter you will learn to use subquery in the following conditions:

- Comparison
- IN
- BETWEEN
- EXISTS
- LIKE
- NULL
- Logical

When you apply a subquery, observe the followings:

- Enclose the subquery in parentheses.
- Do not use a semicolon at the end of the subquery statement.

Comparison condition

If you need to compare to the average of sales prices, you can apply a subquery to compute the average of the sales price as in the following example. In this example, the subquery is on line 4, which returns one value. This kind of subquery, which returns one row and one column, is called **scalar** subquery.

```
SELECT *
FROM sales s
WHERE s.sale_price <=
  (SELECT AVG(sale_price) FROM sales)
;
```

```
1  SELECT *
2    FROM sales s
3    WHERE s.sale_price <=
4      (SELECT AVG(sale_price) FROM sales)
5    ;
```

Note that you can just apply the AVG function as in the following statement.

```
SELECT *
FROM sales s
WHERE s.sale_price <= AVG(s.sale_price)
;
```

```
1  SELECT *
2  FROM sales s
3  WHERE s.sale_price <= AVG(s.sale_price) ;
```

▲▼
📖 Query Result ×

📌 🖨 🔁 📑 SQL | Executing:SELECT *FROM sales sWHERE

```
ORA-00934: group function is not allowed here
00934. 00000 -  "group function is not allowed here"
*Cause:
*Action:
Error at Line: 3 Column: 23
```

As another example, we use a subquery to get the customer_no of a customer based on its name.

```
SELECT *
FROM sales
WHERE customer_no =
  (SELECT customer_no FROM customer
  WHERE customer_name = 'Head Office')
;
```

```
1 ⊟ SELECT *
2   FROM sales
3   WHERE customer_no =
4     (SELECT customer_no FROM customer
5     WHERE customer_name = 'Head Office')
6   ;
```

Note that without the parentheses enclosing the subquery, you will get an error.

```
SELECT *
FROM sales
WHERE customer_no =
```

```
SELECT customer_no FROM customer
WHERE customer_name = 'Head Office'
;
```

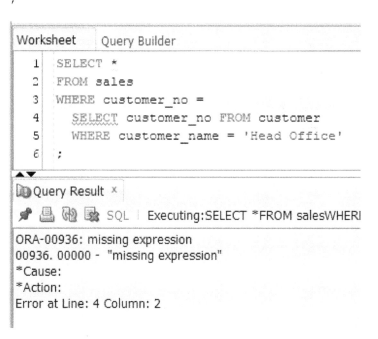

The statement will also fails when you terminate the subquery with a semicolon ;

```
SELECT *
FROM sales
WHERE customer_no =
  (SELECT customer_no FROM customer
  WHERE customer_name = 'Head Office';)
;
```

```
Worksheet    Query Builder
  1   SELECT *
  2   FROM sales
  3   WHERE customer_no =
  4     (SELECT customer_no FROM customer
  5     WHERE customer_name = 'Head Office';)
  6   ;
```

```
Query Result ×   Script Output ×
            Task completed in 0.062 seconds


Error starting at line : 6 in command -

Error report -
Unknown Command
```

Multiple expressions

You can also use subquery in a multiple expression condition as demonstrated in the following example. The subquery is on line 4 - 5.

```
SELECT *
FROM sales
WHERE (product_code, sale_price) =
  (SELECT product_code, price FROM product
  WHERE product_name = 'Go')
;
```

```
Worksheet    Query Builder
  1  SELECT *
  2   FROM sales
  3   WHERE (product_code, sale_price) =
  4     (SELECT product_code, price FROM product
  5     WHERE product_name = 'Go')
  6   ;
```

In the HAVING clause

Similarly, you can use a subquery in the condition of the HAVING clause as in the following example. The subquery is on line 5.

```
SELECT * FROM sales s WHERE EXISTS
(SELECT sales_dt FROM sales
GROUP BY sales_dt
HAVING sales_dt >
(SELECT launch_dt FROM product WHERE product_name = 'R Studio')
)
;
```

```
1 SELECT * FROM sales s WHERE EXISTS
2 (SELECT sales_dt FROM sales
3 GROUP BY sales_dt
4 HAVING sales_dt >
5 (SELECT launch_dt FROM product WHERE product_name = 'R Studio')
6 )
7 ;
```

Group comparison conditions

A subquery can participate in group condition: ANY and ALL. The following statement has a subquery on the > ANY condition.

Worksheet	Query Builder
1	SELECT * FROM sales s
2	WHERE sales_dt > ANY
3	(SELECT launch_dt FROM product)
4	;

Note that without the ANY the statement will fail as the = alone expects a single value (a single row with one column) from the subquery.

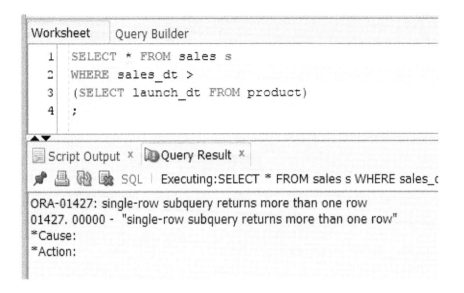

IN Condition

You use the IN condition to compare to a list of values.

In the following example, we would like the sales rows for three products: LINUX, Eclipse, and NetBeans. These three values are supplied by the subquery on line 4 – 6.

```
SELECT *
FROM sales s
WHERE s.product_code IN
  (SELECT product_code
  FROM product
  WHERE product_name IN ('LINUX', 'Eclipse', 'NetBeans')
  );
```

```
1 ⊟ SELECT *
2   FROM sales s
3   WHERE s.product_code IN
4     (SELECT product_code
5     FROM product
6     WHERE product_name IN ('LINUX', 'Eclipse', 'NetBeans')
7     );
```

Expression list

Expressions in the select list of a subquery are evaluated in their specified order.

The subquery on line 4 – 6 provides the values for comparing to product_code and sale_price in this order.

```
SELECT *
FROM sales s
WHERE (s.product_code, s.sale_price ) IN
  (SELECT product_code, price
  FROM product
  WHERE product_name IN ('LINUX', 'Eclipse', 'NetBeans')
  );
```

In the following condition, where the subquery does not provide values in the correct order, the query output will not be as expected.

```
1 ⊟ SELECT *
2   FROM sales s
3   WHERE (s.product_code, s.sale_price )IN
4     (SELECT price, product_code
5     FROM product
6     WHERE product_name IN ('LINUX', 'Eclipse', 'NetBeans')
7     );
```

BETWEEN condition

A BETWEEN condition determines whether the value of one expression is in an interval defined by two other expressions. A subquery can supply any of the two interval values of a BETWEEN condition as demonstrated in the following example, where the lower boundary is the average price and the higher boundary is the maximum price of all products

```
SELECT s.*
FROM sales s
WHERE sale_price BETWEEN
  (SELECT AVG(price) FROM product)
AND
  (SELECT MAX(price)FROM product)
;
```

```
1 ⊟ SELECT s.*
2   FROM sales s
3   WHERE sale_price BETWEEN
4     (SELECT AVG(price) FROM product)
5     AND
6     (SELECT MAX(price) FROM product)
7   ;
```

EXISTS Condition

You can also apply subquery in EXISTS Condition.

```
SELECT *
FROM sales s
WHERE EXISTS
  (SELECT p.price FROM product p
  WHERE product_name LIKE 'R%')
;
```

```
1 ☐ SELECT *
2   FROM sales s
3   WHERE EXISTS
4     (SELECT p.price FROM product p
5     WHERE product_name LIKE 'R%')
6   ;
```

Pattern matching

A subquery can supply a value on any side, or both sides, of a LIKE condition. In the following example the subquery is on the left side of the LIKE.

```
SELECT *
FROM sales s
WHERE
  (SELECT product_name
    FROM product p
    WHERE p.product_code = s.product_code)
  LIKE 'R%';
```

```
Worksheet    Query Builder
1 ☐ SELECT *
2   FROM sales s
3   WHERE
4     (SELECT product_name
5       FROM product p
6       WHERE p.product_code = s.product_code)
7     LIKE 'R%';
```

NULL condition

You can apply subquery in a condition testing for NULL, i.e. whether the query returns any output or not.

The subquery in the following query supplies a value of 1 when the product name starts with R. The value is tested if it is NULL. Only if it does start with R, the sales rows will be returned.

```
SELECT s.*
FROM sales s
WHERE
  (SELECT 1
    FROM product
    WHERE product_name LIKE 'R%'
    AND s.product_code = product_code)
  IS NULL;
```

```
Worksheet    Query Builder
1  SELECT s.*
2   FROM sales s
3   WHERE
4     (SELECT 1
5        FROM product
6        WHERE product_name LIKE 'R%'
7        AND s.product_code = product_code)
8      IS NULL;
```

Logical Condition

A logical condition combines the results of two conditions to produce a single value. A subquery can supply the value of any of the individual condition.

Here is an example with an OR condition. The two subqueries are each on both sides of the OR condition.

```
SELECT *
FROM sales s
WHERE sale_price =
```

```
(SELECT price FROM product WHERE product_code = 1)
 OR
 sale_price     =
(SELECT price FROM product WHERE product_code = 9
);
```

```
1 ⊟ SELECT *
2   FROM sales s
3   WHERE sale_price =
4     (SELECT price FROM product WHERE product_code = 1)
5      OR
6      sale_price     =
7     (SELECT price FROM product WHERE product_code = 9
8     );
```

Chapter 2: Generating Select Lists

The select list of a SELECT statement is the list of expressions before the FROM clause. The expressions are separated by a comma.

```
SELECT expression, expression … FROM …
```

A subquery can be an expression as in the following example. The subquery is the 2nd expression, line 2.

```
SELECT s.product_code,
   (quantity * sale_price) / 10 AS normalized_sales_amt,
   (SELECT price FROM product p WHERE p.product_code = s.product_code) *
       s.quantity / 10
    AS normalized_product_sales_amt
FROM sales s;
```

```
1 ⊟ SELECT s.product_code,
2        (SELECT price FROM product p WHERE p.product_code = s.product_code)
3          * s.quantity / 10 AS normalized_product_sales_amt
4   FROM sales s
5   ;
```

Function parameter

A subquery can also be a parameter of a function. In the following example, our subquery supplies the parameter of the TO_CHAR function.

```
SELECT * FROM sales
WHERE
    product_code =
    TO_CHAR(
    (SELECT product_code FROM product WHERE product_name = 'Go')
    );
```

```
1 ⊟ SELECT * FROM sales
2   WHERE
3        product_code =
4        TO_CHAR(
5        (SELECT product_code FROM product WHERE product_name = 'Go')
6        );
```

Chapter 3: Creating Virtual Table

Consider the following SELECT statement joining two tables, sales and product.

```
SELECT * FROM sales s JOIN product p
ON s.product_code = p.product_code;
```

You can replace the product table with a subquery. The subquery on line 4 – 10 returns a virtual table. In this example, you need product_code and product_name supplied by Big Supplier vendor, which are perfectly returned by the pv (virtual) table generated by the subquery.

```
SELECT * FROM sales s JOIN
(SELECT product_code, product_name, vendor_name
FROM product p JOIN vendor v
ON p.vendor_no = v.vendor_no
WHERE vendor_name = 'Big Supplier') pv
ON s.product_code = pv.product_code;
```

```
 1  SELECT *
 2  FROM sales s
 3  JOIN
 4    (SELECT product_code,
 5       product_name,
 6       vendor_name
 7    FROM product p
 8    JOIN vendor v
 9    ON p.vendor_no    = v.vendor_no
10    WHERE vendor_name = 'Big Supplier') pv
11    ON s.product_code = pv.product_code;
```

Inline View

If you (will) use such a subquery in other statements, you might want to create a view:

```
CREATE VIEW pv AS
(SELECT product_code, product_name, vendor_name
FROM product p JOIN vendor v
ON p.vendor_no = v.vendor_no
```

```
WHERE vendor_name = 'Big Supplier')
;
```

Then, the previous query becomes:

```
SELECT * FROM sales s JOIN pv
ON s.product_code = pv.product_code;
```

If you need the subquery (the view) only in a specific statement you can write it inline as in the statement that needs it, such as in the original query above. That's why such a subquery is also known as **inline view**.

Chapter 4: Facilitating Data Maintenance

CREATE TABLE, INSERT, UPDATE, DELETE, and MERGE statements can have subqueries.

Creating Table

Here is the syntax.

```
CREATE TABLE table_name AS subquery;
```

The following CREATE TABLE statement has a subquery on line 2 -3. A table named last_year_sales will be created and a copy of last year sales rows populated into the table.

```
CREATE TABLE last_year_sales AS
  (SELECT *
    FROM sales
    WHERE TO_CHAR(sales_dt, 'YYYY') = TO_CHAR(TRUNC(sysdate, 'YY') - 1,
      'YYYY')
  )
;
```

```
1 ⊟ CREATE TABLE last_year_sales AS
2     (SELECT * FROM sales
3       WHERE TO_CHAR(sales_dt, 'YYYY') = TO_CHAR(TRUNC(sysdate, 'YY') - 1, 'YYYY') )
4   ;
```

You can create a table with column specifications from some existing tables. The ROWNUM <1 prevents any row to be inserted.

```
CREATE TABLE last_year_sales_empty AS
  (SELECT * FROM sales
    WHERE TO_CHAR(sales_dt, 'YYYY') = TO_CHAR(TRUNC(sysdate, 'YY') - 1,
      'YYYY')
    AND ROWNUM < 1 )
;
```

```
Worksheet    Query Builder
  1 ⊟ CREATE TABLE last_year_sales_empty AS
  2      (SELECT * FROM sales
  3        WHERE TO_CHAR(sales_dt, 'YYYY') = TO_CHAR(TRUNC(sysdate, 'YY') - 1, 'YYYY')
  4        AND ROWNUM < 1 )
  5    ;
```

Adding Rows

The syntax is as follows.

```
INSERT INTO subquery VALUES(…);
```

You can use a subquery to specify the columns where a new row to be inserted. The following example inserts a row into product_code and sale_price columns of the last_year_sales table.

```
INSERT
INTO (SELECT product_code, sale_price
    FROM last_year_sales)
VALUES (99, 99);
```

```
Worksheet    Query Builder
  1 ⊟ INSERT
  2    INTO (SELECT product_code, sale_price
  3          FROM last_year_sales)
  4    VALUES (99, 99);
```

Updating Rows

The syntax is as follows.

```
UPDATE INTO subquery VALUES (subquery);
```

Here is an example.

```
Worksheet    Query Builder
1 ⊟ UPDATE
2     sales
3   SET
4     ( sale_price )
5     =
6     (SELECT p.price
7     FROM product p JOIN sales s
8     ON s.product_code = p.product_code AND p.product_name = 'R Studio'
9     );
```

Notice the syntax that subquery can be on either or both the value to be updated and the updating value. The following example has subquery on both.

```
UPDATE
  (SELECT sale_price
  FROM last_year_sales lys JOIN product p ON lys.product_code =
       p.product_code
  AND product_name = 'R'
  )
SET
  (
    sale_price
  )
  =
  (SELECT p.price
  FROM product p JOIN sales s
  ON s.product_code = p.product_code AND p.product_name = 'R Studio'
  );
```

```
Worksheet    Query Builder
 1   UPDATE
 2     (SELECT sale_price
 3     FROM last_year_sales lys JOIN product p ON lys.product_code = p.product_code
 4     AND product_name = 'R'
 5     )
 6   SET
 7     (
 8        sale_price
 9     )
10     =
11     (SELECT p.price
12     FROM product p JOIN sales s
13     ON s.product_code = p.product_code AND p.product_name = 'R Studio'
14     );
```

Deleting Rows

DELETE FROM subquery WHERE condition;

The condition can be a subquery as well.

The following example has subquery both in the FROM clause and the WHERE condition. We would the UDPATE statement to delete R rows of last_year_sales table if there's any customer name Stranger in the sales table who bought R.

```
DELETE
FROM
  (SELECT 1
  FROM last_year_sales lys
  JOIN product p ON lys.product_code = p.product_code AND product_name =
      'R'
  )
WHERE EXISTS
  (SELECT 1
  FROM customer c JOIN sales s ON c.customer_no = s.customer_no
      JOIN product p ON p.product_code = s.product_code
  WHERE c.customer_name = 'Stranger' AND p.product_name = 'R'
  )
;
```

Worksheet | Query Builder

```
 1 ⊟ DELETE
 2   FROM
 3     (SELECT 1
 4     FROM last_year_sales lys
 5     JOIN product p ON lys.product_code = p.product_code AND product_name = 'R'
 6     )
 7   WHERE EXISTS
 8     (SELECT 1
 9     FROM customer c JOIN sales s ON c.customer_no = s.customer_no
10   JOIN product p ON p.product_code = s.product_code
11     WHERE c.customer_name = 'Stranger' AND p.product_name = 'R'
12     ) ;
```

Chapter 5: Defining View

Effectively, a view is a pre-defined query, and the pre-defined query is a subquery (as it's a query in an SQL statement)
Here is the syntax.

```
CREATE VIEW view_name AS (subquery)
```

And, here is an example. The subquery is on line 2 – 5.

```
CREATE or replace view pv AS
(SELECT p.product_code, p.product_name, v.vendor_name
FROM product p JOIN vendor v
ON p.vendor_no = v.vendor_no
WHERE v.vendor_name = 'Big Supplier')
;
```

```
Worksheet    Query Builder

 1 ⊟ CREATE VIEW pv AS
 2   (SELECT p.product_code, p.product_name, v.vendor_name
 3   FROM product p JOIN vendor v
 4   ON p.vendor_no = v.vendor_no
 5   WHERE v.vendor_name = 'Big Supplier')
 6   ;
```

Materialized View

Similar to view, you also use subquery when creating materialized view.

The syntax is.

```
CREATE MATERIALIZED VIEW mv_name AS (subquery)
```

And, as an example.

```
CREATE MATERIALIZED VIEW mpv AS
(SELECT p.product_code, p.product_name, v.vendor_name
FROM product p JOIN vendor v
ON p.vendor_no = v.vendor_no
WHERE v.vendor_name = 'Big Supplier')
;
```

Worksheet	Query Builder

```
1 CREATE MATERIALIZED VIEW mpv AS
2  (SELECT p.product_code, p.product_name, v.vendor_name
3  FROM product p JOIN vendor v
4  ON p.vendor_no = v.vendor_no
5  WHERE v.vendor_name = 'Big Supplier')
6  ;
```

Chapter 6: Factoring

You can factor a subquery using the WITH clause preceding the statement that uses the factored subquery.

WITH subquery_name AS (SELECT...

The following statement creates the factored big_supp, which is then used in the SELECT statement that follows the factored subquery. The subquery is on line 2 – 9.

```
WITH big_supp AS
(SELECT p.product_code,
        p.product_name,
        v.vendor_name
    FROM product p
        JOIN vendor v
        ON p.vendor_no = v.vendor_no
    WHERE v.vendor_name = 'Big Supplier'
)
SELECT s.*, big_supp.*
FROM sales s join big_supp on
s.product_code = big_supp.product_code
;
```

```
 1 WITH big_supp AS
 2 (SELECT p.product_code,
 3         p.product_name,
 4         v.vendor_name
 5     FROM product p
 6         JOIN vendor v
 7         ON p.vendor_no = v.vendor_no
 8     WHERE v.vendor_name = 'Big Supplier'
 9 )
10 SELECT s.*, big_supp.*
11 FROM sales s join big_supp on
12 s.product_code = big_supp.product_code
13 ;
```

Chapter 7: Correlated Subquery

A subquery that references its parent's column(s) is a correlated subquery.

Here's an example. The correlated subquery on line 4 – 6 references the customer_no column of its parent s.customer_no column.

```
SELECT *
FROM sales s
WHERE customer_no =
  (SELECT customer_no FROM customer c
  WHERE s.customer_no = c.customer_no
  AND customer_name = 'Quality Store')
;
```

```
1 ⊟ SELECT *
2   FROM sales s
3   WHERE customer_no =
4     (SELECT customer_no FROM customer c
5     WHERE s.customer_no = c.customer_no
6     AND customer_name = 'Quality Store')
7   ;
```

Here is an example correlated subquery in the select list. The correlated subquery is on line 2.

```
SELECT s.product_code,
    (SELECT price FROM product p WHERE p.product_code = s.product_code)
    * s.quantity / 10
    AS normalized_product_sales_amt
FROM sales s;
```

```
1 ⊟ SELECT s.product_code,
2     (SELECT price FROM product p WHERE p.product_code = s.product_code)
3     * s.quantity / 10
4     AS normalized_product_sales_amt
5   FROM sales s;
```

You can also apply a subquery on the ORDER BY clause.

```
SELECT s.*
FROM sales s
ORDER BY
  (SELECT p.vendor_no
  FROM product p
  WHERE s.product_code = p.product_code
  )
;
```

```
1 ⊟ SELECT s.*
2   FROM sales s
3   ORDER BY
4     (SELECT p.vendor_no
5     FROM product p
6     WHERE s.product_code = p.product_code
7     )
8   ;
```

A correlated subquery as a virtual table (in the FROM clause) is not allowed, as the parent's table(s) is not visible to the subquery.

```
SELECT s.product,
SELECT * FROM sales s JOIN
(SELECT product_code, product_name, vendor_name
FROM product p JOIN vendor v
ON p.vendor_no = v.vendor_no
AND s.product_code = p.product_code
WHERE vendor_name = 'Big Supplier') pv
ON s.product_code = pv.product_code;
```

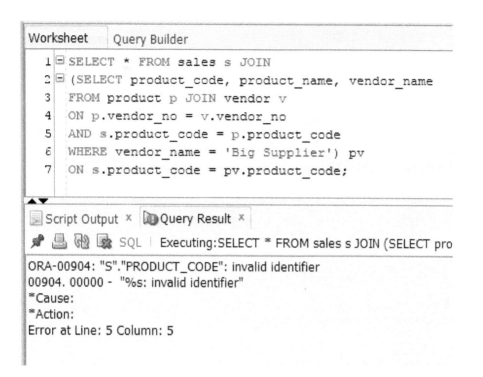

Worksheet | Query Builder

```
1 □ SELECT * FROM sales s JOIN
2 □ (SELECT product_code, product_name, vendor_name
3   FROM product p JOIN vendor v
4   ON p.vendor_no = v.vendor_no
5   AND s.product_code = p.product_code
6   WHERE vendor_name = 'Big Supplier') pv
7   ON s.product_code = pv.product_code;
```

Script Output ×   Query Result ×

SQL | Executing:SELECT * FROM sales s JOIN (SELECT pro

```
ORA-00904: "S"."PRODUCT_CODE": invalid identifier
00904. 00000 -  "%s: invalid identifier"
*Cause:
*Action:
Error at Line: 5 Column: 5
```

Chapter 8: Multilevel Subquery

A subquery can contain another subquery. The following example has two levels. The first level is on line 4 – 6. The second level is on line 7 – 10.

Note that you can access higher level query's column. In the example, the second level subquery accesses its grandparent's customer_no column on line 9.

```
SELECT s.*
FROM sales s
WHERE EXISTS
  (SELECT 1
  FROM product p
  WHERE p.product_code = s.product_code AND EXISTS
    (SELECT 1
    FROM customer c
    WHERE c.customer_no = s.customer_no
    )
  ) ;
```

```
 1  SELECT s.*
 2    FROM sales s
 3    WHERE EXISTS
 4      (SELECT 1
 5      FROM product p
 6      WHERE p.product_code = s.product_code AND EXISTS
 7        (SELECT 1
 8        FROM customer c
 9        WHERE c.customer_no = s.customer_no
10        )
11      ) ;
```

Chapter 9: In the Set Operators

When you write a statement that has set operator(s), the part of the statement are subqueries.

The following example statement that has a UNION operator has two subqueries participating. Both subqueries have second level subquery.

```
SELECT *
FROM sales s
WHERE s.sale_price <=
  (SELECT AVG(sale_price) FROM sales)
UNION
SELECT *
FROM sales s
WHERE s.sale_price BETWEEN 5 AND
(SELECT AVG(sale_price) FROM sales)
;
```

Appendix A: Setting Up

This first chapter is a guide to install and set up the Oracle Database 11g Expression Edition release 2 and SQL Developer version 4. Both are available at the Oracle website for download at no charge.

Installing Database Express Edition

Go to http://www.oracle.com/technetwork/indexes/downloads/index.html

Locate and download the Windows version of the Oracle Database Express Edition (XE). You will be requested to accept the license agreement. If you don't have one, create an account; it's free.

Unzip the downloaded file to a folder in your local drive, and then, double-click the setup.exe file.

You will see the Welcome window.

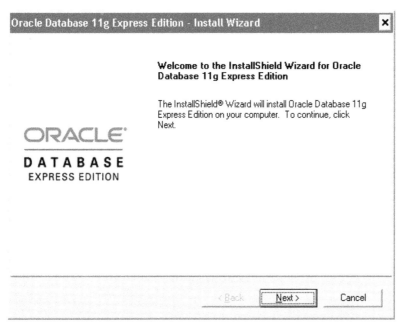

Click the Next> button, accept the agreement on the License Agreement window, and then click the Next> button again.

The next window is the "Choose Destination Location" window.

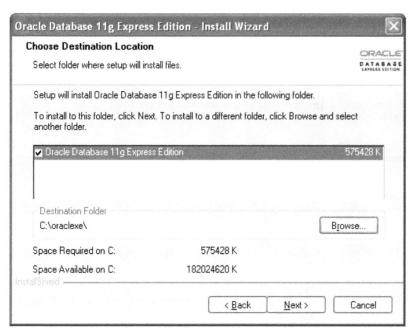

Accept the destination folder shown, or click the Browse button to choose a different folder for your installation, and then click the Next> button.

On the prompt for port numbers, accept the defaults, and then click the Next> button.

On the Passwords window, enter a password of your choice and confirm it, and then click the Next> button. The SYS and SYSTEM accounts created during this installation are for the database operation and administration, respectively. Note the password; you will use the SYSTEM account and its password for creating your own account, which you use for trying the examples.

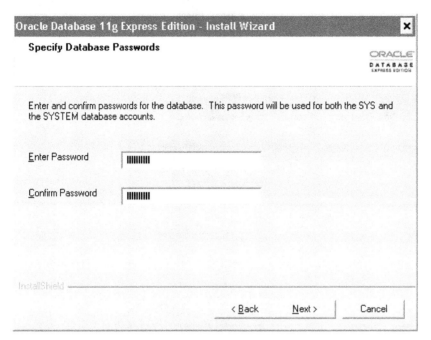

The Summary window will be displayed. Click Install.

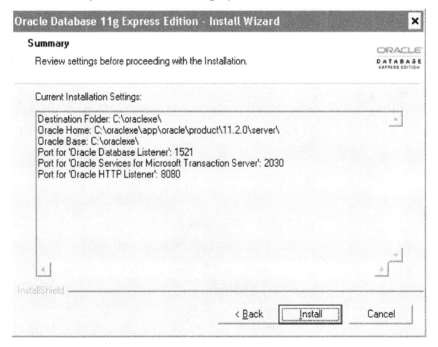

Finally, when the Installation Completion window appears, click the Finish button.

Your Oracle Database XE is now installed.

Installing SQL Developer

Go to http://www.oracle.com/technetwork/indexes/downloads/index.html

Locate and download the SQL Developer. You will be requested to accept the license agreement. If you don't have one, create an account; it's free.

Unzip the downloaded file to a folder of your preference. Note the folder name and its location; you will need to know them to start your SQL Developer.

When the unzipping is completed, look for the sqldeveloper.exe file.

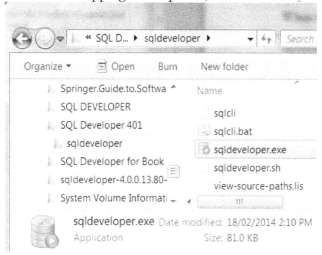

You start SQL Developer by opening (double-clicking) this file.

You might want to create a short-cut on your Desktop.

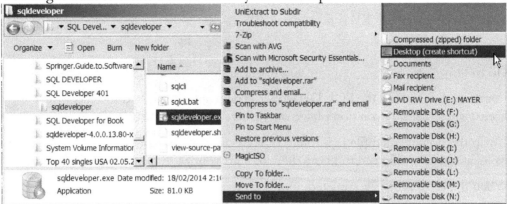

You can then start your SQL Developer by double-clicking the short-cut.

Your initial screen should look like the following. If you don't want to see the Start Page tab the next time you start SQL Developer, un-check the *Show on Startup* box at the bottom left side of the screen.

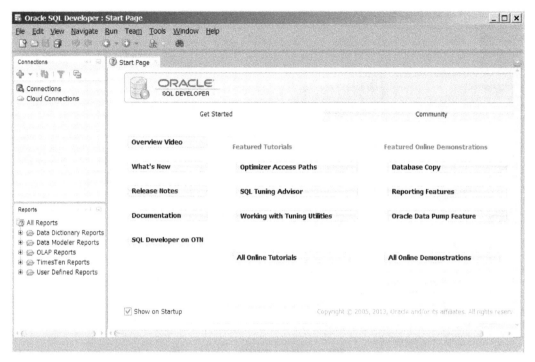

For now, close the Start Page tab by clicking its x.

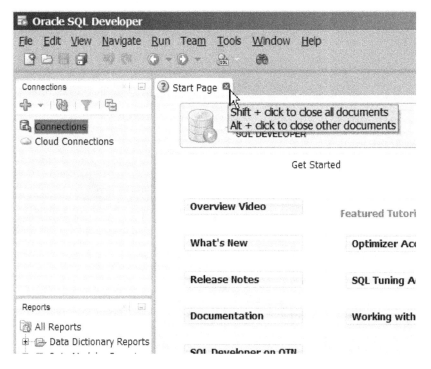

Creating Connection

To work with a database from SQL Developer, you need to have a connection.

A connection is specific to an account. As we will use the SYSTEM account to create your own account, you first have to create a connection for the SYSTEM account.

To create a connection, right-click the Connection folder.

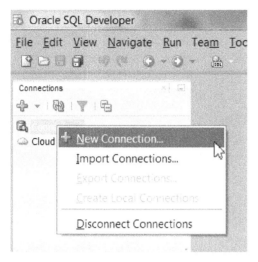

On the New/Select Database Connection window, enter a Connection Name and Username as shown. The Password is the password of SYSTEM account you entered during the Oracle database installation. Check the Save Password box.

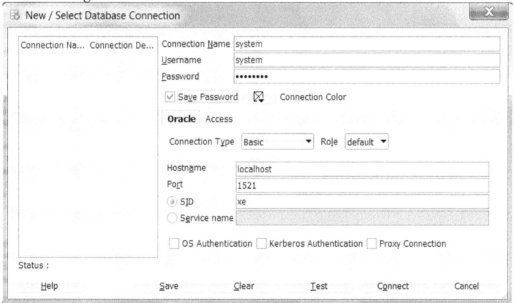

When you click the Connect button, the *system* connection you have just created should be available on the Connection Navigator.

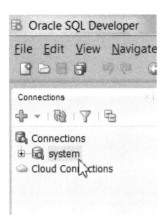

A Worksheet is opened for the system connection. The Worksheet is where you type in source codes.

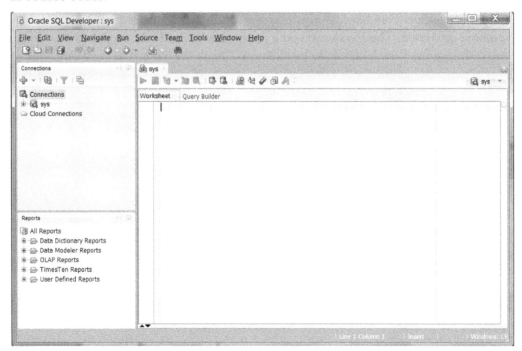

Creating Database Account

You will use your own database account (user) to try the book examples.

To create a new account, expand the system connection and locate the Other Users folder at the bottom of the folder tree.

Right click and select Create User.

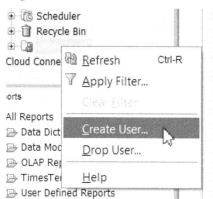

Enter a User Name of your choice, a password and its confirmation, and then click the Apply button. You should get a successful pop-up window; close it.

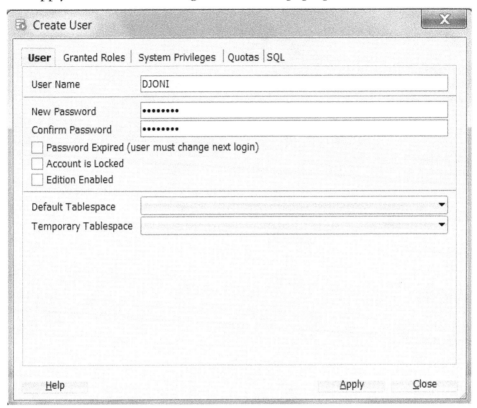

On the Granted Roles tab, click Grant All, Admin All and Default All buttons; then click the Apply button. Close the successful window and the Edit User as well.

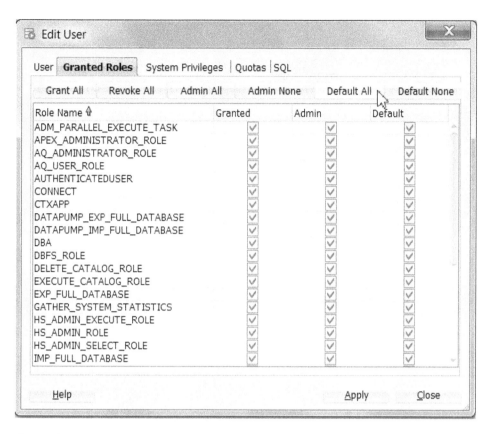

Creating Your Connection

Similar to when you created system connection earlier, now create a connection for your account.

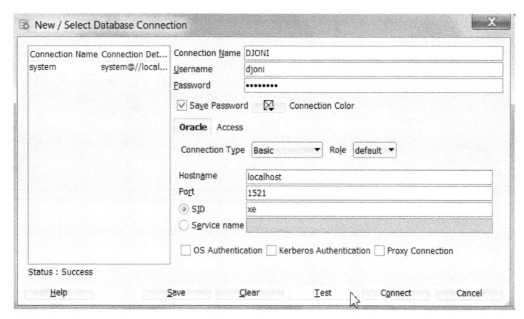

Click the Connect button. A worksheet for your connection is opened (which is *DJONI* in my case).

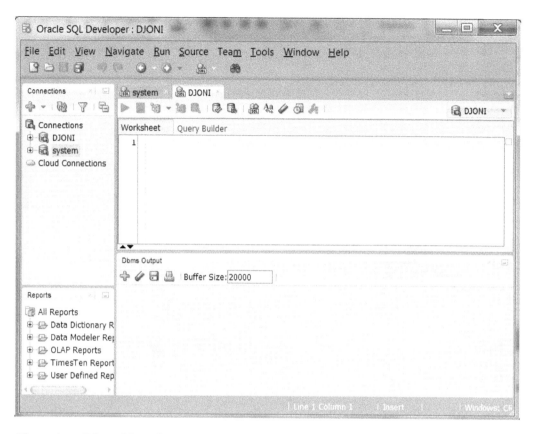

Showing Line Numbers

In describing the book examples I sometimes refer to the line numbers of the
program; these are line numbers on the worksheet. To show line numbers, click
Preferences from the Tools menu.

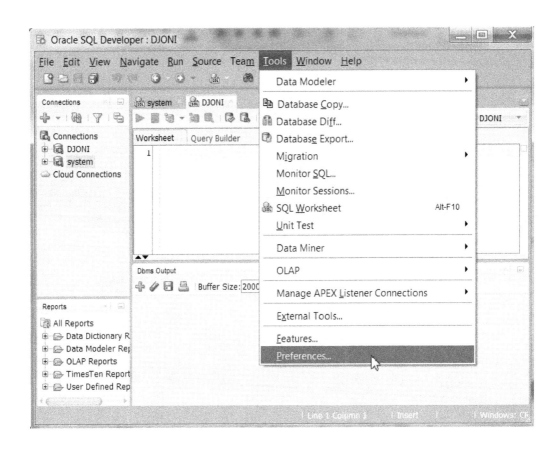

Select Line Gutter, then check the Show Line Numbers. Your Preferences should look like the following. Click the OK button.

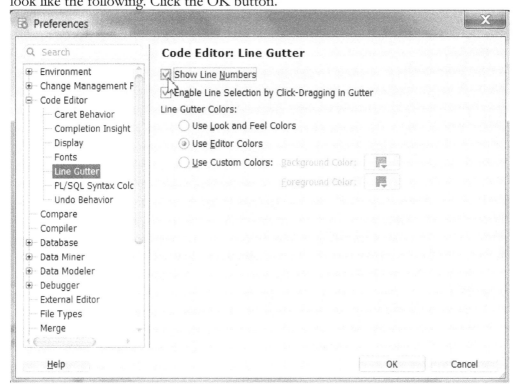

Deleting the *system* Connection

Delete the *system* connection, making sure you don't use this account mistakenly. Click Yes when you are prompted to confirm the deletion. Your SQL Developer is now set.

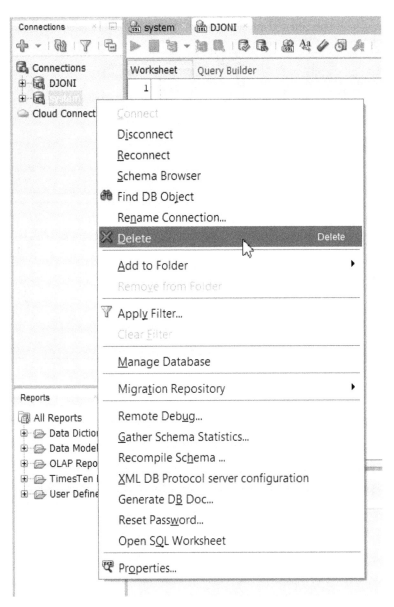

Close the *system* worksheet.

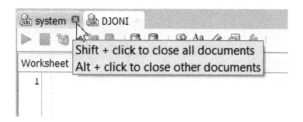

49

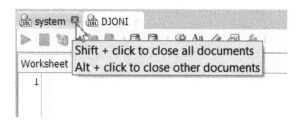

Appendix B: Using SQL Developer

This chapter shows you how to use the SQL Developer features that you will use to try the book examples.

Entering SQL statement

The worksheet is where you enter SQL statement.

Start your SQL Developer if you have not done so. To open a worksheet for your connection, click the + (folder expansion) or double-click the connection name. Alternatively, right-click the connection and click Connect.

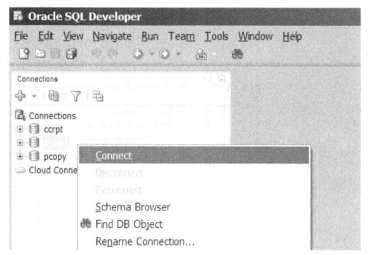

Note the name of the worksheet (tab label) is the name of your connection.

You can type source code on the worksheet.

Appendix A has the source code of all the book examples. Instead of typing, you can copy a source code and paste it on the worksheet.

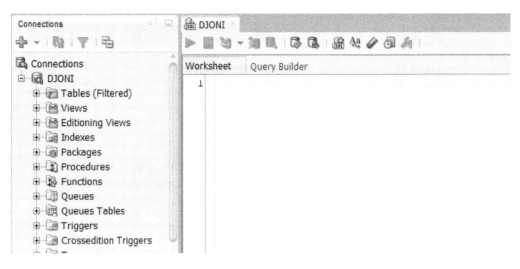

SQL Statement

Some of the book examples use a table named *produce*. Type in the SQL CREATE TABLE statement shown below to create the table (you might prefer to copy the *create_produce.sql* listing from Appendix A and paste it on your worksheet)

You run a SQL statement already in a worksheet by clicking the Run Statement button.

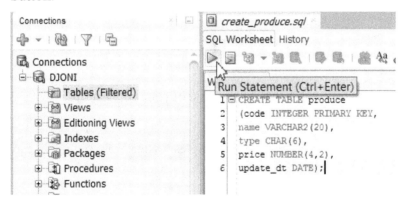

The Script Output pane confirms that the table has been created, and you should see the produce table in the Connection Navigator under your connection folder. If you don't see the newly created table, click Refresh.

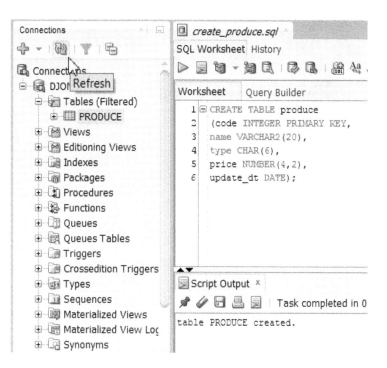

Inserting Rows

As an example of running multiple SQL statements in SQL Developer, the following five statements insert five rows into the produce table. Please type the statements, or copy it from *insert_produce.sql* in Appendix A. You will use these rows when you try the book examples.

Run all statements by clicking the Run Script button, or Ctrl+Enter (press and hold Ctrl button then click Enter button)

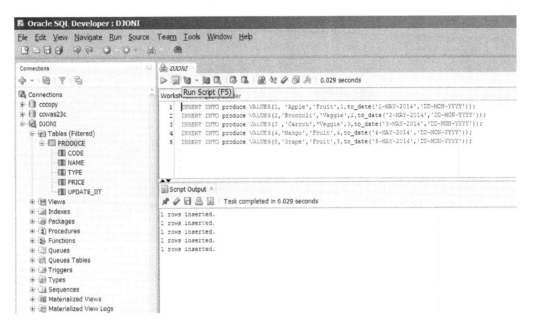

Multiple worksheets for a connection

Sometimes you need to have two or more programs on different worksheets. You can open more than one worksheet for a connection by right-clicking the connection and select Open SQL Worksheet.

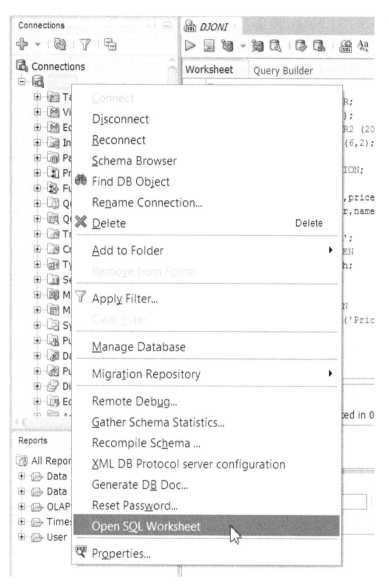

The names of the next tabs for a connection have sequential numbers added.

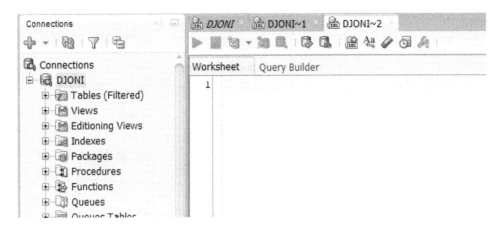

Storing the source code

You can store a source code into a text file for later re-opening by selecting Save from the File menu.

Select the location where you want to store the source code and give the file a name, and then click Save.

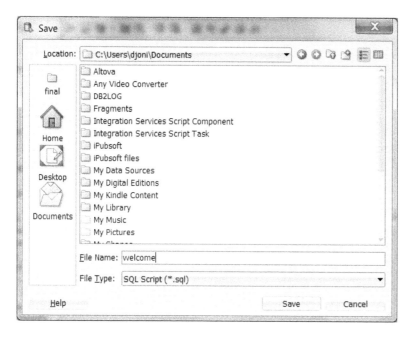

Opening a source code

You can open a source code by selecting Open or Reopen from the File menu and then select the file that contains the source code.

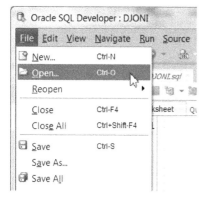

The source code will be opened on a new worksheet. The tab of the worksheet has the name of the file. The following is the worksheet opened for the source code stored as file named running_plsql.sql.

Running SQL from a file

You can execute a file that contains SQL statement without opening it on the worksheet as shown here.

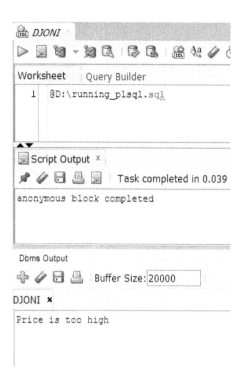

Clearing a Worksheet

To clear a Worksheet, click its Clear button.

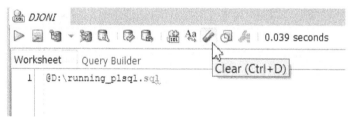

Index

www.ingramcontent.com/pod-product-compliance
Lightning Source LLC
Chambersburg PA
CBHW082112070326
40689CB00052B/4610